For The Hell Of It.
Jo-Anne Pigram.

ISBN 978-1-300-03077-5
July, 2012.
Copyright (c) 2012 Jo-Anne Pigram
All rights reserved. No part of this publication may be reproduced or transmitted in any form, or by any other means, electronically or mechanically, including photocopy, recording or any information storage and retrieval system, without permission in writing from the author.

For The Hell Of It.
This book is not dedicated to anyone and serves no real purpose.
There is really no good reason for this book.
This book was written for no other reason, other than because I wanted to, because I felt like it.
Because I could – for the hell of it.

Sweety

I lay the afternoon to waste
and we lay and I dream of your face.
The sky changes, blue, mauve, grey and black.
Isn't it funny how opposites attract?

You lay next to me.
I can hear you breath -
In, out and in, out again and again.
Your heart beat is intense.

I can feel your pulse with only centimetres between us -
pounding the beat of lust.
I feel the warmth of the air from your mouth against me.
I get high on the smell of your breath. I am your deeply devoted debauchee.

Your chest rises and falls.
You flutter, shiver, shake. Almost nervous.
The hair on your chest trembles with the beat of your heart.
You seem afraid that I am about to eat you – Sweety.

Craving.

You are that shady character -
that has just what I need.
But there's a barrier I have to overcome,
I need to succeed.
I'm staring blankly at you, struck dumb.

You are jaw dropping
and lip smackingly
BEAUTIFUL.
I am drooling.
Oh! Who am I fooling?

You got what I need, everything I could ever want.
I'm like an addict for speed. Hooked.
I'm acting like a deviant, a delinquent.
It's worse than I feared and better than I had hoped.
I'm suffering and enjoying every minute of this derangement.

I'm obsessed and I can't concentrate.
I get so frustrated.
Thinking about you all the time
like it's some crime.

Because you are jaw dropping
and lip smackingly
BEAUTIFL.
I am drooling.
Oh! Who am I fooling?

Broken Non-Promises

Hope I haven't kept you waiting long.
Time ticks on. Minutes roll in to days, hourly.
Hope you're not wrong.
'cause I'm late and you jumped the gun. Fell, felt way too early.

Only to be sure I have to keep the pace.
A second chance, after a a weak minute.
Only because of a pretty face.
Tempted into letting go because you are too cute.

I fell for it again.
You said you were sorry but laughed behind my back and under your breath you gave off a blood gurgling scream.
I stabbed you in the jugular vein.
You didn't know what I mean.

I said it's ok alright, it doesn't hurt at all.
The dogs bark isn't as bad as it's bite.
I guess it could hurt a little more.
But you're being so polite.

You tell me how you'd rather die than hurt a hair on my head.
But you do, an action says more than a word
Swearing that isn't what you said.
That's exactly what I heard.

I said I'd think about it, give me time.
I said I needed space to sort through this.
I gave you a line.
You gave me this.

Confusion.
It's not abused till it's over used.
My confession.
I never thought I'd lose.

Time Will Tell

Tomorrow
shall improve yesterday
and go careening in to the past.
To extend upon the story.
The kind that happens only in sleep
when the sun and the moon share kisses,
between the dawn of a new days sunrise
whilst I dream away.

Because you had been there

The intensity simmered
in the heat of the summer.
My skin blushed
because he had been there.
Skin sun kissed by him.
Goosebumps raised on smooth flesh.
His touch echoes deep within
as my heart beat pounds his name.
The music to his song.

Save the Last Chance for Me.

Driving off lonely in to the rain.
Defeated.
Left wanting, still without.
I'm used to the consistent disappointment.
Admiration amidst despair
I forget in fascination
I could not deny myself
one last shivering dance
outside in the cold with you.

<3 You.

Walking along the pavement
after a tasteless dance.
Inspired by my rotten imaginaton.
My wanting frailty.
I delved from weakness in to temptation.
Overstepping faithfulness' boundary
into depravity.
My heart is still yours.

Aftermath

How can I recognise love after you dropped the bomb
ensuring utter chaos
would tear my life apart.
Turn me around.
I choose conscious awareness.
I choose to know.
I chose sadness, death, frailty.
I chose to cry. I could have laughed
like thunder
following me down to your level.
The calls you made
bought me knowledge,
bought me back down to earth.

I will never be the same again.

I Am.

My confidence was disturbed with anxious frailty.
Goodbye.
It has since been replaced by bravery.
Strength.
A compassionate sense of understanding for myself.
I sparkle in light of what you shed upon me.
The knowledge of how you perceive me.
Yes I am all that.

Tra – La – La – La – La.

We lay, my head nestled in your smooth bare arms.
I can hear the pounding of your heartbeat screaming out my name.
Your voice is low, deep, relaxed.
Eyes half closed.
You kiss my forehead
whisper music to my ears.
"I love you."
Your heartbeat is caught in your voice on your breath.
A symphony of all my favourite sounds.

Honesty

Your tongue dances along your teeth,
an idea comes to mind.
One too obscene to share.
I dare not share my deepest darkest fantasies with you.

Illusion

You are before me, as beautiful as ever before.
Undressed in your Sunday best.
My heart skips a beat.
I breathe deeper, softly.
As if trying to hold on to the words that want to escape.
I close my eyes, praying that they will not spill out between my lips.
But they do.
I tell you to your face, all I've ever wanted to say.
All my dreams come true in an instant.

How a Memory is Made.

A night on the town
turns in to something more.
An innocent passer by,
becomes a not so innocent memory
when eyes meet - shot across a room,
The looks which see
linger on in the night air.
Long after the breeze has left.
Your presence fills the air around me.
Like perfume.
A scent to remember you
as you walk by in to my past.
All it takes is a smirk, a smile.
A hello.
Too much talking.
Laughter, giggles.
Careless embraces.
You are like the after taste of champagne.
Once my lips leave the glass,
my senses become full of you
A taste lingers.
A taste that turns in to drunkeness,
into dancing.
A taste that turns into a memory.

What's His Name?

I am at liberty to forget
the fine lines drawn
that I am dangerously dancing between
wisdom wonders
What's his name?
I'm at liberty to forget
He exsists for a moment.

He looks like you
handsome.
Tall dark mysterious.
Tomorrow shall decide
once you stop whispering in my ear
cooing idosynchrasies

I listen encouragingly
purring enchanted.
Obedient to the hungry thrill
of faithless comfort found
underneath underwear.

Everything we said we shall not do.
When we said I do.
In sickness and in health
till death do us part.
I'm love sick and he would kill me.

I Want To. I Want You.

The weakness within
makes me shiver.
My eyes glaze over and
whisper to you -
screaming "I need you".

Fueling the Fire

Time begins to interefere
when I want you here.
Too bad. Luck is tough.
Hope is never enough.
Luck is cruel
when you are the fuel.
To the passion I contain, the fire burning within.
When my heart pounds the beat of sin.

Faithfully Yours

Too caught up in the heat of the moment and strangled by the gold binding their hands.
Clasps around their fingers laced together with wedding bands.
Freedom is first lost with early fools.
As if it's precious jewels
have been stolen when eyelashes beat the heart.
Stolen from the start.

The Danger of Strangers

Who is he?
I don't know him.
He looks good, smells good, tastes good.
He HAS to be good.
<moment later/different angle/lighting/music/drink/sobriety/day/night/only a one night stand –
or a possible divorce waiting to happen?>
WOW! Was I mistaken!
Yeah, I was Miss Taken when I first laid eyes on him.
Miss taken identity!
Miss taken for granted – Maybe!
Miss Understood. Yes? No?
YES!

I believe you are Mr Right and well how do I say this nicely.
Ummmmmmmmmmmmmmmmmm
"Sorry, I must have been mistaken
- I thought you were Mr Perfect".

Speechless

Spelling It Out A, B, C and D.

Amorous.
Biased Toward.
Caring.
Dazzled.
Excited.
Fluttering heartbeat.
Gorgeous.
High.
Inviting.
Joyous,
Kiss,
Longing.
Mania.
Nostalgia.
Orgasmic.
Quixotic.
Sexy.
Titillated.
Understated.
Valentine.
Wishful.
XXXXXXX Rated.
Yearning.
Zeal.

Through/To Hell with You.

Me and my army.
That's who.
Death is too kind.
Jail a rotten repayment.
All I owe you is misery.
A perfect match.
For the likes of you.

www.ingramcontent.com/pod-product-compliance
Lightning Source LLC
Chambersburg PA
CBHW080409170426
43193CB00016B/2866